# Explaining
# the
# Holy Spirit

## Bob Gordon

Sovereign World

Sovereign World Ltd
PO Box 777
Tonbridge
Kent TN11 0ZS
England

Unless otherwise indicated, all scripture quotations are from the New International Version, inclusive language version. © Copyright the International Bible Society 1999, published by Hodder and Stoughton.

ISBN 1 85240 335 7

The publishers aim to produce books which will help to extend and build up the Kingdom of God. We do not necessarily agree with every view expressed by the author, or with every interpretation of Scripture expressed. We expect each reader to make his/her judgment in the light of their own understanding of God's Word and in an attitude of Christian love and fellowship.

Cover design by CCD, www.ccdgroup.co.uk
Typeset by CRB Associates, Reepham, Norfolk
Printed in the United States of America

# Contents

# 1

# The reality of the Holy Spirit

The discovery of the personality and power of the Holy Spirit is a tremendous experience for any person.

Like me, some have been believers for many years before knowing at first hand the vibrancy of the Spirit's presence. When I opened myself to the indwelling fullness of the "divine guest," however, I found a new dimension of the Christian life.

The implications of that event have been far reaching, and in some instances, costly. I have discovered pain in the Spirit as well as deep joy. Yet as I look back on all those years, I will never regret having come to know and accept this gift.

Some people experience the fullness of the Holy Spirit as soon as they first commit themselves to God. Unlike others, they are not hindered by suspicion and traditional attitudes from being open to his presence.

Yet all of us who have received the Spirit discover what Jesus meant when he said,

> *Whoever believes in me, as the Scripture has said, will have streams of living water flowing from within.* (John 7:38)

There is something inadequate about trying to explain the Holy Spirit. Both the Bible and our experience make it clear that there is much more to him than can ever be fully defined. Images in Scripture like fire, water and wind actually add to the sense of mystery.

Time and again we are told that the Spirit's work is not to

5

disclose himself, but to reveal Jesus. On one hand he is "God in the present tense," but on the other hand he is the divine incognito. He comes not to draw attention to himself, but to make the work of God more complete in our lives.

## Two witnesses

Although there are many aspects of the Spirit's work, his actions fall mainly into two categories.

First, he brings us to an awareness of God through the work of inner conviction. Jesus speaks of this in John 16:8:

> *When he comes, he will convict the world of guilt in regard to sin and righteousness and judgment.*

In his discussions with the Jewish teacher Nicodemus, Jesus described believers as *"everyone born of the Spirit"* (John 3:8). He used the graphic picture of birth to describe the spiritual change taking place for anyone who responds to this initial work of the Holy Spirit.

We need to be clear at the outset that there is no such thing as a true Christian believer without the Holy Spirit. Of course, not all Christians live in conscious openness every day to the Spirit. But we cannot become Christians apart from the work of the Holy Spirit, who opens our eyes to our own need and to the tremendous gift of God in Jesus Christ.

Paul uses a different picture to emphasize the work of the Holy Spirit in salvation. Not only does the Spirit bring us *to* God, he keeps us *in* God!

> *Having believed, you were marked in him with a seal, the promised Holy Spirit, who is a deposit guaranteeing our inheritance until the redemption of those who are in God's possession – to the praise of his glory.* (Ephesians 1:13–14)

Therefore there is an inner testimony of the Holy Spirit in the heart of each person who through faith believes in God.

*And this is the testimony: God has given us eternal life, and this life is in his Son.*                                    (1 John 5:11)

*The Spirit himself testifies with our spirit that we are God's children.*                                             (Romans 8:16)

The first activity of the Holy Spirit in our lives, then, is to bring us to a place of faith, show us our need for God and reveal to us God's love in Jesus Christ.

This is a basic truth. Over the years I have met people who claim to have experienced the Holy Spirit, but seem to have little or no experience of personal salvation. Some of them even object to the very suggestion that we all need to experience this new birth in Christ. But the Bible is unequivocal: without it we are still outside the life of God!

The second major area of the Holy Spirit's activity occurs when we have become Christians. Just as we could never come to God without the Spirit's help, we could not live a Christian life apart from his help.

This work in the believer's life is the main emphasis of this booklet. It is clear that there are many Christians in the same state that I was. They believe in God. They have made a confession of faith. They care about truth and upright living and faithfulness to God. Yet there is something missing.

These believers have never known that personal infilling of the Holy Spirit. They themselves would say that their Christian lives lack power. They long for a greater sense of openness and freedom in their own spirits. They may also confess to a lack of victory in deep personal or relational areas of their lives.

If that sounds familiar, then this booklet is written for you.

## The anointing of Christ

We have already seen how Paul speaks of the initial work of the Holy Spirit in the life of every believer (Ephesians 1). The Spirit is the inward witness and guarantee of the new life into which we have been brought through faith in Jesus.

Later in the same letter, Paul goes on to express his desire that:

*I pray that out of his glorious riches he may strengthen you with power through his Spirit in your inner being, so that Christ may dwell in your hearts through faith.*          (Ephesians 3:16–17)

This verse became very real to my wife as she was seeking answers to her own spiritual need. When she read these words, it suddenly dawned on her that although she was a committed Christian, there was something else she needed to experience from God.

She needed to know in a deep, inward and personal way the infilling strength of the Holy Spirit. Notice what Paul says: *"so that Christ may dwell in your hearts through faith."*

The name *Christ* is very significant here. It means in Greek "the anointed one," just like the Hebrew word *messiah.* Jesus is the anointed one, the one with God's power. He showed this in his ministry on earth as he brought the power of God's kingdom into the lives of hopeless, sick, defeated people. He *"anoints"* those who believe in him, so that out of their lives will pour the same living water (John 7:38).

Hebrews 1:3 tells us that Jesus is now ascended and at the Father's right hand waiting to come again in glory. How, then, are we to experience his "Christing," the reality of his power? How can we experience the same anointing as Jesus? It is through the indwelling power of the Holy Spirit.

Jesus himself made that clear to his disciples when he said:

*I will ask the Father, and he will give you another Counselor to be with you for ever – the Spirit of truth. The world cannot accept him, because it neither sees him nor knows him. But you know him, for he lives with you and will be in you.*   (John 14:16–17)

## Signs of the Spirit

Despite the deep mysteries concerning the Holy Spirit, there is a sheer simplicity and exuberance about his work in a person's life. I remember clearly the day I first experienced the infilling of the Spirit. There was a sense of surprise, joy, relief, anticipation and a fresh knowledge of God's presence.

I look back with some wistfulness to these hallmarks of the Spirit's first entrance. As years go by we often tend to become so sophisticated in our approach to spiritual matters that we lose that original vitality, the spark which is the essence of his presence.

Many people would characterize the baptism of the Spirit quite narrowly, identifying it with the ability to speak in tongues or other phenomenon. It is certainly true that these signs occur when a person is touched by the Spirit of God, but the issue is wider and deeper. When we encounter the Spirit of God, he brings us into the depths, the holiness, and the power of God. These are greater than any manifestation, because they have to do with God's very nature.

Six important elements stand out as the universal hallmarks of the Holy Spirit.

## 1. A sense of God himself

The Holy Spirit brings God to us, and brings us to God. This is what happened when the prophet Isaiah was overwhelmed by the awareness of God in the temple at Jerusalem. In an authentic experience of the Holy Spirit, our primary attention is not on the gifts or any particular emotional experience. We become aware of God himself!

Out of this awareness flow streams of emotion, strength, gifting, and so on. But at the heart is God. There is a core sense of his majesty. What a great God he is!

It was this profound sense of God that gripped the disciples on the day of Pentecost. After the outpouring of the Holy Spirit, *"everyone was filled with awe"* (Acts 2:43).

## 2. The dynamic reality of God's power

The word most associated with the Holy Spirit in Scripture is power. God can do anything and in him we can do all things. Paul wrote, *"I can do everything through him who gives me strength"* (Philippians 4:23).

The sense of power doesn't grow out of our own inflated ego, but the humbling realization of the capacity of God. Our God is omnipotent – all-powerful – and he wants to infuse his all-surpassing power into the weakness of our humanity (2 Corinthians 4:7).

### 3. The immediacy of the kingdom

Through the Spirit, we can know God here and now. His rule extends right to the heart of our own experience. This is why Jesus said to the Pharisees that *"the kingdom of God is within you"* (Luke 17:21).

The Holy Spirit is God in the present tense, right inside our life situations, communicating with us, opening himself up to us and looking for us to open ourselves to him in response.

### 4. The gifts of the Holy Spirit

Each time that we read in the New Testament about the outpouring of the Spirit, there are manifestations of the gifts as well.

Before I encountered the Holy Spirit, the subject of spiritual gifts had been taboo. My upbringing and theological pre-conditioning had closed my mind to such things. But when the Spirit came, so did his gifts (see 1 Corinthians 12). Some came suddenly and others more gradually, but through the years there has been a continual opening up to more and more of the gifts.

### 5. An upsurge of praise and worship

The Holy Spirit lifts our hearts up to God, and inspires our minds and imaginations to express the greatness and love of God. Through him we understand what it means to offer a *"sacrifice of praise – the fruit of lips that confess his name"* (Hebrews 13:15). This may have been foreign to us before, but through the release of the Spirit we find ourselves overflowing with thankfulness and worship. Just as David sang and danced before the Lord, there is a spontaneous response when the Spirit touches us.

## 6. Unity of heart and spirit

In the past, I would join with other believers only on the ground of doctrinal agreement, denominational affiliations or other fairly external factors. When I experienced the Holy Spirit in a new way, however, I was immediately brought into a new and larger place of fellowship. For the first time in my life I felt uninhibited in expressing my oneness with fellow travelers in faith.

This is a major feature of the work of the Spirit, which many have lost. Doctrine and truth are important, but we must cherish unity in the body of Christ as we hold these things.

Some people argue about the meaning of terms like "baptism in the Spirit," "being filled with the Spirit," or being "sealed in the Spirit." Yet terminology is secondary to the reality of our need of God. We can only enter into more of his presence through the inward work of the Holy Spirit.

Others argue about timing. Do we need to wait a while after conversion, or do we receive the Holy Spirit when we first confess Christ? God's timing is the crucial thing. If God speaks to you, then don't hold back, answer him. If you are spiritually thirsty, then come and drink.

Our need is met in God's heart. God wants to give us the Spirit so that we may know him better and experience his *"incomparably great power for us who believe"* (Ephesians 1:18).

# 2

# Person to person

The Holy Spirit is a Person – with a capital "P"! He is not a vague influence or mystical idea. It is from him that all our own personhood flows. Paul said,

> *I kneel before the Father, from whom his whole family in heaven and earth derives its name.* (Ephesians 3:14–15)

Because God is a Person who created us as persons in his image, we share some very important things in common. He can communicate and make himself real to us. We cannot necessarily see him, but he can make a great impression on our lives through our inner selves.

Even among human beings, though superficial contact depends partly on sight, our deeper and more lasting encounters with each other are based on contacting the inner person. When our spirits are stirred, something profound takes place, making a lasting impact.

As persons we have a capacity to either open or close our inner beings to each other. We do it every day of our lives, whether meeting people, watching television, or responding to objects and circumstances. We open or close ourselves as feels appropriate, allowing ourselves to be affected to varying degrees.

If you were walking down the street and spotted someone you really disliked, what would you do? Most of us wouldn't just ignore him and cut him dead. We would shake hands and smile or nod politely, yet at the same time shut ourselves off from a genuine personal encounter.

Yet suppose you saw someone coming in the distance who you admire greatly. There may be the same handshake and similar conversation, but something very different would take place. It may only be for a minute or two, with a fleeting glance or a warm word but there can be a sense of personal contact. If you and the other person are opened inwardly to each other, there can be a deep spiritual meeting. As you go your separate ways, it seems as though part of you goes with him, and part of him goes with you.

Because God is a Person, he has the same capacity to open himself in a situation, or to withhold himself. Our own capacity to do this is a pale shadow of his! Just as deeper encounters between human beings often begin with small things, so it is with God. He often speaks in quiet, personal ways. Sometimes he has a special word through something we hear or read, perhaps in the Scriptures. He whispers to us in our circumstances, and shouts to us in our pain. God is not short of ways to make us aware that he has something to say. He is a Person and he speaks to us personally.

## Living water

The Bible also describes the Holy Spirit using the image of water. Jesus said that whoever believes in him *"will have streams of living water flowing from within"* (John 7:38). He was telling us that every believer would know the reality of the Holy Spirit, bringing life and strength into the center of their being. The Bible makes it clear that without this, God's power cannot flow out into our daily lives. The gift of the Spirit is absolutely necessary for the full enjoyment and fulfillment of our human existence.

Our lives can be compared to drinking glasses. Just as these are made specifically to hold water, the purpose of our lives is to hold God! God created us to be the channels of his life here on earth. He wants us to live and operate in that power for the good of the whole of creation. The first two chapters of Genesis exemplify this.

God's great plan for the human race was spoiled when Adam and Eve failed to appreciate their great privilege and purpose in representing him. Because of sin we can no longer hold the power of God in our lives. We are leaking vessels. Without God's help, we can't contain the living power of the Holy Spirit.

Think of a smeared, dirty glass. We wouldn't offer anyone a drink of water in such a thing. It needs to be washed thoroughly and rinsed clean before it is usable. God has made it possible, through Jesus, for our lives to be cleansed of all their filth inside. Some of us look spotless on the outside but need deep cleansing in our hearts. Remember,

> *The* LORD *does not look at the things people look at. Human beings look at the outward appearance, but the* LORD *looks at the heart.* (1 Samuel 16:7)

Or maybe the glass is cracked, with large chips in it. We would throw such a glass away. In the same way, many people feel worthless before God and other people because of their "cracks." The circumstances of their lives have dealt them severe blows from which they feel unable to recover. Yet God has a tender way with such people, and is able to touch them and make them whole. Jesus exemplified this. He said, *"It is not the healthy who need a doctor, but the sick"* (Matthew 9:12).

Throughout his ministry on earth, Jesus healed those whose lives were damaged by sickness and disability, loneliness and hurt. He then sent them out with a new strength, no longer needing to live in their infirmity. God wants to do this for each one of us! He brings us healing and forgiveness in the cross, and then fills us with his life and power through the Holy Spirit.

Glasses are made to be filled. A glass that has never held water has never served the purpose for which it was designed. We are also made to be filled. If we have never known the fullness of

God's power through the Holy Spirit, we have never fulfilled the purposed for which we were created. God is waiting to fill us with himself.

Of course, it's impossible to fill a glass that is turned upside down all the time! Water may flow for hours out of the faucet but if the glass is upside down, it will remain empty. So it is with us: we need to be open and "right side up" for God to fill us. We need to be willing in our spirits to receive the Spirit of God. Just as we invite other people into our lives at a deeper level, we also need to invite the Holy Spirit more deeply into our lives. He will not force his way in.

## Power unlimited

There are four important reasons why we all need the power of the Holy Spirit in our lives:

### 1. Power to become

Without the power of God in us we can never become children of God. Some people imagine that because we are born naturally into the world, we are thereby children of God. Yes, that is God's original intention, but we have all fallen from right recognition of our true Father. In the words of Isaiah,

> *We all, like sheep, have gone astray,*
> *each of us has turned to our own way.*          (Isaiah 53:6)

But God has made a way home for every one of us, and it's the Holy Spirit's job to bring us back. As we have already seen, he awakens our spiritual need and points us to Jesus. John tells us in his gospel,

> *To all who received him, to those who believed in his name, he*
> *gave the right to become children of God – children born not of*
> *natural descent, nor of human decision or a husband's will, but*
> *born of God.*          (John 1:12–13)

The Greek word translated "right" in that verse is *exousia*, which means "power" or "authority." The power of the Holy Spirit does in us what we could never do for ourselves. We can become God's children and truly live as members of his family.

## 2. Power to be

Because the Holy Spirit is dwelling in us, we have the power that we need for daily living. It is a great thing to be born again by the Holy Spirit, but we must continue as living examples of Jesus day by day. Because of the weakness of our flesh, we need the Spirit's power to do this.

The prayer of the apostle Paul addresses this very issue:

> *I pray that out of his glorious riches he may strengthen you with power through his Spirit in your inner being.*
>
> (Ephesians 3:16)

We don't have to live the Christian life in our own strength. God has opened to us the channel of divine power. The amazing fact is that God himself wants to dwell in our hearts! Like us, the Christians at Corinth were struggling in a demanding world, open to the temptations of the flesh. Paul challenged them, saying:

> *Do you not know that your body is a temple of the Holy Spirit, who is in you, whom you have received from God? You are not your own; you were bought with a price. Therefore glorify God with your bodies.* (1 Corinthians 6:19–20)

## 3. Power to overcome

Every Christian believer lives in a war zone. We can't escape that. When we chose to follow Jesus, we changed sides. The Bible makes it clear that every human being is governed at a spiritual level by some power or other. If we are not living with Jesus as our Lord then we are surely living under the domination of some other spiritual power:

> *As for you, you were dead in your transgressions and sins, in*
> *which you used to live when you followed the ways of this world*
> *and of the ruler of the kingdom of the air, the spirit who is now*
> *at work in those who are disobedient.*          (Ephesians 2:1–2)

When we become Christians, the battle can become fierce. It can seem as though the warfare becomes much tougher after we believe, because Satan increases his attack on us to prevent us from following Jesus. The great difference is that we are now on the winning side! God makes his power available within us so that we have the knowledge and strength to defeat the enemy. John says:

> *You, dear children, are from God and have overcome them,*
> *because the one who is in you is greater than the one who is in*
> *the world.*          (1 John 4:4)

## 4. Power to share

The Holy Spirit came with great power on the gathered disciples at Pentecost. The whole house was filled with the noise of a mighty wind, and what seemed like tongues of fire came and rested on every one of them. What an experience that must have been!

The risen Jesus had already prophesied of the Spirit's coming:

> *You will receive power when the Holy Spirit comes on you; and*
> *you will be my witnesses in Jerusalem, and in all Judea and*
> *Samaria, and to the ends of the earth.*          (Acts 1:8)

The word used here for power is different from the one we looked at before. This word is *dunamis*, from which we get our English word "dynamite." That's power! Because the Holy Spirit came like dynamite, the disciples too were able to be like dynamite, as is clear in a reading of the Acts of the Apostles. They went all over the world, and wherever they went, God's kingdom came in power.

This is what God wants today! He wants our lives to be so filled with the power of the Holy Spirit that we will be dynamite. We are to be true witnesses to the life of Jesus, not only speaking about him to others but doing his works. It is what Jesus promised would happen:

> *I tell you the truth, anyone who has faith in me will do what I have been doing. He will do even greater things than these, because I am going to the Father.*                  (John 14:12)

# 3

# Majesty and mercy

The Holy Spirit reveals to us the nature of our holy God. God's holiness is intrinsic to him, and we can never understand holiness apart from his self-revelation.

When God reveals his holy nature, what we see is glory. This is illustrated time and again in the Scriptures. As Moses went up the mountain to receive the law, the glory of the Lord settled on Mount Sinai and appeared as a consuming fire (Exodus 24:16–17). God's glory appeared in the tabernacle during the wilderness journey of the children of Israel, as for example in Leviticus 9:23. The same thing happened when Solomon dedicated the temple in Jerusalem (1 Kings 8:11).

This language of glory is used at the beginning of John's gospel of the coming of Jesus in the world:

> *The Word became flesh and made his dwelling among us. We have seen his glory, the glory of the One and Only, who came from the Father, full of grace and truth.* (John 1:14)

When we encounter the glory of God we begin to comprehend something of his nature. He is wholly Other. He is different. And his aim is to make us different!

Paul beautifully expresses this process of holiness in 2 Corinthians 3:18:

> *And we, who with unveiled faces all reflect the Lord's glory, are being transformed into his likeness with ever-increasing glory, which comes from the Lord, who is the Spirit.*

It is through witnessing the glory of God that we are able to reflect both his glory and his holiness.

## Encounter with God

Isaiah had a very deep revelation of the holiness of God. This is his testimony:

> *In the year that King Uzziah died, I saw the Lord seated on a throne, high and exalted, and the train of his robe filled the temple. Above him were seraphs, each with six wings: With two wings they covered their faces, with two they covered their feet, and with two they were flying. And they were calling to one another:*

> > *"Holy, holy, holy is the Lord Almighty; the whole earth is filled with his glory."*

> *At the sound of their voices the doorposts and thresholds shook and the temple was filled with smoke.*
> *"Woe to me!" I cried. "I am ruined! For I am a man of unclean lips, and I live among a people of unclean lips, and my eyes have seen the King, the Lord Almighty."*
> *Then one of the seraphs flew to me with a live coal in his hand, which he had taken with tongs from the altar. With it he touched my mouth and said, "See, this has touched your lips; your guilt is taken away and your sin atoned for."*
> *Then I heard the voice of the Lord saying, "Whom shall I send? And who will go for us?"*
> *And I said, "Here I am. Send me!"*            (Isaiah 6:1–8)

These words convey an experience of such power and depth that few of us have ever known it. To be touched by God's fire, to know that you have escaped from death under the blazing glory of Almighty God, challenges all of life.

Isaiah's vision of God is beyond understanding. The prophet is trying to express something for which no words are adequate. Nevertheless, we sorely need to perceive it ourselves.

There was a moment in my own life when those words became absolutely real for me. I encountered God in some small measure of the living power of which Isaiah speaks. Even now, years later, although I have denied it many times by my sinful actions, that experience lives vividly in my heart and mind. It would not be exaggerating to claim that it has become the very foundation of my whole life and work.

God's heart desire is that we should enter into a deep understanding and fellowship with him. This experience of his holiness and power is not the exclusive privilege of members of some inner group or secret sect. It is available to all believers who will open their hearts and seek him, though too few of us truly do so.

We all need this experience of being taken into the heart of God. We need to know his purity, his love, and his jealousy. I am not speaking of petty human jealousy, but divine jealousy, passionately concerned with righteousness and justice, the very cornerstone of his nature.

We need to feel the greatness of God's heart, so that we will be delivered from the smallness of our own hearts. We need to hear his heartbeat, so that our own hearts will beat with it. We need to comprehend as God comprehends, and feel his passion for the exiled and lost.

## Consuming fire

We need to know God's fire. This is what Isaiah encountered in such a devastating way. The live coal that burnt his lips also seared his soul. This was not just a dream, but a profound inward experience of the reality of God. The awesome power of it left the prophet as good as dead – without the touch of the angel he would have been finished.

This is what we need. We need to know that we have come to the absolute end. We need to know the full extent of sin in us and in the world. We need to come to the realization that we would be dead apart from the grace and mercy of God.

Too much modern spiritual experience is of our own making,

superficial and self-centered. We struggle feebly with sin and bondages because we know little of God's power or holiness. Yet in true conversion, we touch the altar of God and find our bonds are burned away.

It is the blazing fire of God's presence that consumes everything of the old life. Nothing less will suffice to deliver us from the self-centered, problem-orientated religion into which many of us have fallen. The Holy Spirit comes to lead us into the heart of God, for that is where spiritual birth takes place and we are radically changed.

The prophet Jeremiah spoke a word to a captive people, which the Holy Spirit wants to declare to you:

> *"You will seek me and find me when you seek me with all your heart. I will be found by you," declares the* Lord, *"and will bring you back from captivity."*　　　　　　　　(Jeremiah 29:13–14)

## Baptism of fire

Many people speak of the baptism of the Holy Spirit as if it were a little movement of joy, leading to gifts such as speaking in tongues. These explanations have led people to seek the gifts and not the Giver himself. Yet a face-to-face encounter with the reality, holiness and power of God is a baptism of fire.

God starts the process by causing a divine dissatisfaction to unsettle us. It is not in our human nature to turn to God and seek him with all our hearts (Romans 3:11). This stirring within us is prompted by the Holy Spirit. Although we may not recognize his hand, God can use many different means to rouse us from our complacency.

This went on for over two years in my own life when I was a young minister, shortly out of college. I had started research for a PhD and had a privileged position in a university church. If I played my cards right I would do well in my denomination and college, yet I began to feel depressed and dissatisfied with life as it was.

God surrounded me with people who challenged me greatly. There was something in their life which I knew I didn't have, and I became increasingly aware of my need for it.

I began to long deeply for effective power in my daily ministry, particularly among the students I pastored. It was obvious that the old formulae would not work by themselves: no matter how good and true my words were, they needed to be clothed with power.

Eventually a minister friend invited me to attend a residential conference for church leaders on the theme of Holy Spirit renewal. It was a rather staid group of Scottish Presbyterians that had gathered, and I remember little of the first two days, which seemed quite harmless.

## The hand of God

On the final evening, however, an Anglican priest spoke on chapter 6 of Isaiah. I recall much less of what he *said* than what he *was* – a living presentation of his message. It was as though the glory of the Lord shone through him. As I looked at him I knew that this man was living in the good and the wealth of what he was sharing.

I was sitting in a low armchair, but the longer this minister spoke, the more I began to sink into the chair. I felt the hand of God was weighing upon my life. Although I didn't have conviction of any particular sin, I felt as if a tremendous heaviness had descended upon me through the roof of the building, like the weight of the whole world resting on me.

By the time this man finished I felt as though I had disappeared down through the chair onto the floor – even as if I was below the floor! It was a strange, amazing sensation which I find hard to put into words. The talk finished and everyone left the room, but I remained, still sitting there as the darkness of the night drew in.

I knew first-hand what Isaiah meant when he said he was lost and ruined. I felt as though my personal inner world had come to an end. I had become newly aware of God's holiness and power, his purity and judgment. It was like being struck by a twenty-ton truck. There was an overwhelming sense of the light of God's presence, but the brighter this light shone, the more I felt myself overcome by the darkness that is sin in the presence of absolute purity.

## The touch of mercy

After a while my friend and the conference leader came upstairs and looked at me where I sat. Eventually they laid hands on my head, prayed for me and then led me downstairs where others were having supper. I sat there, stunned and silent.

The touch of these men must have been like the angel's touch for Isaiah. I felt the tide turning – I was being permitted to live and not die.

Much later I came across a verse in the apocryphal book of Ecclesiasticus. It says: *"As is his majesty, so too is his mercy."* Praise God, there is only one thing as great as the majesty and holiness of God, and that is his mercy. His love overpowers his wrath in the hearts of those who turn to him.

I went to bed, still trembling and faint. But the next morning when I woke, I pulled back the curtains just as the sun was rising over the hills. It was as though the sun of righteousness had risen with healing in its wings (Malachi 4:2). I was a new creation. It was like being born again all over again! There were depths of God that I had never known before in my whole Christian life. It was as though the fire of the Holy Spirit had been kindled in my heart, and instead of being consumed by it, I had caught it.

After a communion service that morning, I set off to drive home – a journey I will never forget. The Holy Spirit brought songs into my heart and onto my lips that I had never learned. It was as if all the discouragements of the Christian life, those that Satan would try to destroy us with, were nothing compared to the holy joy I felt now. Even the sheep on the hills seemed to gaze in amazement!

The following Sunday I stood to preach in my church and could only share what God had done. It was the start of a completely new and radical phase of my ministry, in which many other people found the power of God.

# 4

# The lamp of the Lord

A special relationship between the Holy Spirit and our inner being seems to be perfectly summed up in the New King James Version of Proverbs 20:27:

> *The spirit of a man is the lamp of the LORD,*
> *searching all the inner depths of his heart.*

We see this also in the alternative translation footnoted in the New International Version:

> *The human spirit is the LORD's lamp;*
> *it searches out the inmost being.*

This introduces us to a dynamic idea of how the transforming power of God is relayed to our personalities. The Holy Spirit makes an impression on our own spirit, which in turn radiates the light and truth of God throughout our being.

Paul's words from 1 Corinthians 3:18, which we have already looked at, also express this truth:

> *And we, who with unveiled faces all reflect the Lord's glory, are being transformed into his likeness with ever-increasing glory, which comes from the Lord, who is the Spirit.*

This means that the Holy Spirit takes what is from the heart of God himself and shines it into our spirits. Here is the transforming power of God, taking us on a process of change by which we can ever increasingly reflect the character of God.

## Divine receiver

Our spirit, which is made alive to God through new birth, becomes the divine receiver through which divine truth and power are relayed into our lives. The exciting fact is that every one of us has the potential in our inner being to receive good things from God.

The Holy Spirit is the one who takes the attributes of God and reflects them into the very heart of our being, our spirits. By means of this Spirit-to-spirit communication, we come to know the deep things of God that would otherwise be locked out of our sphere of experience.

Paul says:

> *"No eye has seen,*
> *no ear has heard,*
> *no mind has conceived*
> *what God has prepared for those who love him" –*
>
> *but God has revealed it to us by his Spirit.*
>
> (1 Corinthians 2:9–10)

If we understand that our spirits are like the lamp of God, we see why the work of the Holy Spirit is not to be interpreted too lightly. We cannot just equate the baptism in the Spirit with the ability to speak in tongues. This gift is important, but the work of the Holy Spirit is more than this. He takes what is found in the very heart of God and makes it real in our own lives.

Through the work of the Holy Spirit, we can begin to participate in the life of God himself. It does not make us gods or mini-gods, as some people have suggested. Rather, what the Holy Spirit does is to re-establish that connection with the divine life that was broken through sin and disobedience, and to restore in us the image of our Creator.

# From the heart of God

We can now look at some of the most important aspects of this divine connection.

## 1. Spiritual understanding

In the second chapter of 1 Corinthians, Paul speaks at length about spiritual wisdom. He describes the Holy Spirit as the one who understands the thoughts of God and reveals them to us.

> *We have not received the spirit of the world but the Spirit who is from God, that we may understand what God has freely given us.* (1 Corinthians 2:12)

Wisdom is an attribute of God, and regarded very highly in the Bible. Divine insight, not human reason or intelligence, was a hallmark of the Messiah (Isaiah 11:2–3), and a sign of the work of the Holy Spirit in our lives.

The function of wisdom is not only to understand the truth of the gospel. Spiritual wisdom helps us to act in God's way and to see into everyday situations through the eyes of the Holy Spirit. The person living in the light of divine wisdom will not be easily diverted from the truth of God or fooled by false spiritual claims.

James recognized the importance of this gift when he said:

> *If any of you lacks wisdom, he should ask God, who gives generously to all without finding fault, and it will be given to him.* (James 1:5)

## 2. The glory of God

God's glory is one of the most dynamic themes in Scripture. From cover to cover the Bible speaks of the glory of God. John connects it with the appearance of Jesus, who manifested the very essence of the character of God. He says:

*We have seen his glory, the glory of the One and Only, who came
from the Father full of grace and truth.*            (John 1:14)

Glory is the outshining of God. Whenever God chooses to
reveal himself, the result is glory. In the experience of Moses
and the children of Israel, God's glory appeared as a physical
manifestation accompanied by other phenomenon such as
smoke and fire.

Likewise, when God is absent there is no glory. When the ark
of the covenant was captured in battle (1 Samuel 4), Eli the
priest and his two sons, Phinehas and Hophni, died under
divine judgment, along with thirty thousand foot soldiers of
Israel. On that dark day, the wife of Phinehas gave birth to a son
and died. She first named the boy Ichabod, which means *"the
glory has departed."*

God's holiness belongs to him alone. We cannot acquire
holiness through keeping rules or obeying laws, however
diligently. To become like God we must experience the impact
of his Person. This can only happen through the Holy Spirit
who shines into our lives with the glory of God, so transforming
our characters.

That is why the secret of holiness is relationship with God
rather than fulfillment of the law. It shows us the great
difference between the new and the old covenants. If we drift
away from God, our backsliding is much more than a failure to
keep rules. It is the failure of a relationship.

### 3. The love of God

Paul highlights the way the Holy Spirit brings God's love to us
as part of his work:

> *God has poured out his love into our hearts by the Holy Spirit,
> whom he has given us.*            (Romans 5:5)

This love of God has very little to do with romantic sentiment-
ality. It is the most healing and revolutionary force in the

universe. Paul said that where the Spirit of the Lord is, there is liberty (2 Corinthians 3:17). There is no fear or bondage in God's love. This love leads to freedom from self-condemnation and the clawing neurosis and fear that so often afflict our personalities. So John says:

> *There is no fear in love. But perfect love drives out fear, because fear has to do with punishment.* (1 John 4:18)

See the power of love to cast out fear, darkness and phobias from our minds and hearts. Because this is true, nothing in all creation can separate us from the love of God that is in Christ Jesus our Lord (Romans 8:39).

God is love, and the Spirit of God brings the nature of God to our own spirits. Here lies the secret of the healing power of the Spirit: he sheds abroad the love of God which is so strong that nothing can overwhelm it. The Song of Songs puts it this way:

> *Place me like a seal over your heart...*
> *for love is as strong as death,*
> *its jealousy unyielding as the grave.*
> *It burns like blazing fire,*
> *like a mighty flame.*
> *Many waters cannot quench love;*
> *rivers cannot wash it away.*
> *If one were to give*
> *all the wealth of one's house for love,*
> *it would be utterly scorned.* (Song of Songs 8:6–7)

## 4. The will of God

Our God is a God of purpose. He is working his own purposes out, and he has a purpose for our lives. This is why Paul prays,

> *Asking God to fill you with the knowledge of his will through all spiritual wisdom and understanding. And we pray this in order*

> *that you may live a life worthy of the Lord and may please him*
> *in every way.*                                    (Colossians 1:9–10)

/ I believe that the inner witness of the Holy Spirit is the most important way that any person can discern God's will. Others can advise and correct, but in the end we each need to recognize the Spirit's guidance. If Jesus is the Shepherd, the Spirit could be compared to a sheepdog nudging us this way and that, bringing us to the place of best fruitfulness in our lives. /

Most of us today are too busy listening to all the other voices around us to be able to perceive clearly the will of God. Because of this, much time and energy is expended on efforts far removed from the perfect will of God for our lives.

Listening to God in the realm of our spirit is a practiced art. But it is not a one-sided affair. The Holy Spirit is beside us, counseling us and gently revealing the will and purpose of God into our spirits.

## 5. The power of God

Power belongs to the Lord. All authority and might find their source in the heart of God. Every other power is a pale reflection and imitation of that original creative power in the hand of God. Through this power he brought everything into being and with the same creative power he recreates our hearts, bringing forgiveness and restoration into our lives.

David the king discovered that long ago when he cried out of his own distress:

> *Create in me a pure heart, O God,*
> *and renew a steadfast spirit within me.*          (Psalm 51:10)

The word *"create"* in that verse is from the very same Hebrew word used to describe the creation of the universe. God did what no one else can do – he created something out of nothing. And he does the same in our lives. Through the power of the creative Spirit he creates new life in us where there was no life.

God then allows us to participate in his power. Paul says:

> *I keep asking that the God of our Lord Jesus Christ, the glorious Father, may give you the Spirit of wisdom and revelation, so that you may know him better. I pray also that the eyes of your heart may be enlightened in order that you may know the hope to which he has called you ... and his incomparably great power for us who believe.* (Ephesians 1:17–19)

Paul goes on to describe the nature of this power:

> *That power is like the working of his mighty strength, which he exerted in Christ when he raised him from the dead and seated him at his right hand in the heavenly realms...*
> (Ephesians 1:19–20)

Whereas before we may have been inclined to say "I can't!" now, in the power of the Holy Spirit, we can affirm that we can do all things through God who gives us strength.

## 6. The peace of God

Jesus came as the Prince of Peace, and he imparted to us the gift of peace.

> *Peace I leave with you; my peace I give you.* (John 14:27)

Peace in this sense means more than an absence of war. It is a positive reality rather than a passive state. God himself is peace because he is one. There is no division or breakdown within his Person, only wholeness. The peace of God can stand guard over our emotions and the anxieties of our mind (Philippians 4:7). Once more, it is made real in our hearts through the Holy Spirit.

> *May the God of hope fill you with all joy and peace as you trust in him, so that you may overflow with hope by the power of the Holy Spirit.* (Romans 15:13)

## 7. The assurance of eternal life

Jesus came to give us God's kind of life, everlasting life. Eternal life is a quality of life that begins now – we don't have to die to experience it. It is the product of the Holy Spirit dwelling in us, through whom we share in the very life of God. That's what Jesus means when he says:

> *I have come that they might have life, and have it to the full.*
> (John 10:10)

But there is also a future dimension to this life. The life we have here and now in the fullness of God will go on forever. This is our hope, the hope of heaven.

We have no proof of eternal life here or then apart from the witness of the Holy Spirit. He is spoken of time and time again as the *"guarantee"* in our hearts of God's promise.

> *Now it is God who has made us for this very purpose and has given us the Spirit as a deposit, guaranteeing what is to come.*
> (2 Corinthians 5:5)

We can begin to grasp the tremendous potentiality of the Holy Spirit in our lives. It is not a matter of a little blessing or occasional spiritual gift. Instead, it is to do with being changed into the likeness and character of our heavenly Father: to know his freedom, to experience his love, to share his wisdom, to live in his power and to abound in his hope.

This puts the question of being open to the Holy Spirit on a completely different plane. It is not just for a special-interest group in the church. Instead, it is a matter of first priority and urgency for every believer to be open to God in this way.

# 5

# Gifts and graces

## The fruit of the Spirit

There are two aspects of the Holy Spirit that must always be kept in balance in our lives. The first is what Paul calls the fruit of the Spirit. These are the qualities established in us that are in line with the character of God. The fruit of the Spirit is the evidence of the work of the Holy Spirit, changing us into the likeness of Jesus.

It is vital that we are bearing fruit in this way. We know from the New Testament church at Corinth that it is possible to have spectacular power gifts alongside grievous sin such as back-biting and division, lust and sexual immorality. These things are a contradiction to the believer's confession of faith. Paul had to remind the church of the need to match their gifts with holiness of life.

God's fruit in our lives is real beauty in a world of degradation and ugliness.

> *The fruit of the Spirit is love, joy, peace, patience, kindness, goodness, faithfulness, gentleness and self-control.*
> (Galatians 5:22–23)

Can you imagine the effect within society if we all actively pursued these attributes in our daily behavior? These are not weak, irrelevant qualities but characteristics of God with the power to bring healing and life in a world of death.

When we bear this fruit, we have divine strength to reject hatred, pride and self-interest, violence and evil. It takes all the power of the Spirit to enable us to live in the kindness, goodness, patience and love of God. These things are foreign to our unredeemed human nature, but as we are filled with the Spirit they supplant the traits of our old nature.

> *Therefore, if anyone is in Christ, there is a new creation: the old has gone, the new has come!*　　　　　　(2 Corinthians 5:17)

## The gifts of God

The gifts of the Holy Spirit are supernatural endowments beyond our natural talents. This is not to denigrate our natural abilities! People who have taken the time and trouble to train in a profession, or who have special skills and aptitudes, are of great use in the service of God's kingdom.

Nevertheless, the gifts of the Spirit are of a different order. They are not the result of training or expertise, although it is possible to develop them through use. They are just as available to the uneducated as well as to those of great intellectual prowess.

It is true that those who are very intellectually oriented may have more trouble in receiving them. All of us tend to want to do things in our own strength, but when it comes to the gifts of the Spirit they can only be received in humble submission to God.

Some of us have explained away the idea of spiritual gifts altogether. There is a theological position that these things occurred at the beginning of the Christian era as a temporary sign, and died out soon after. Perhaps for some Christians it is more comfortable not to have to expect these rather bizarre events to occur now. Yet there is no scriptural justification for such a position.

Others have reacted against what were seen as extremes in certain sections of the church. Sadly, the baby has been thrown out with the bath water and some believers have been left unaware that the gifts of the Spirit are available today. This means that many faithful Christians have been bereft of tools to enhance their faith, deepen their worship, and equip them for daily life and witness among people in need.

## Given to give away

There are three important passages of Scripture that provide an overview of the gifts of the Spirit: Romans 12:3–8, 1 Corinthians 12, and Ephesians 4:7–16. They show the great variety of spiritual gifts. Some are for private use, and others suited to a congregational setting. Most are for very practical purposes, whereas others manifest the supernatural power and glory of God through faith, healing, miracles and the like.

Whatever their character, they have in common that they are inspired and distributed by the Holy Spirit. He is the source of all of the gifts, and they are given freely to all who ask.

> *The Spirit's presence is shown in some way in each person for the good of all.*        (1 Corinthians 12:7, Good News Bible)

The exciting thing about the gifts of the Spirit is that they are given to us so that we can give them away! We receive these spiritual capacities so that the power of God can be shared in the lives of other people.

## Trinitarian gifts

Chapter 12 of 1 Corinthians is the central passage regarding the spiritual gifts. Yet it shows us that the phrase "gifts of the Holy Spirit" is in some ways misleading. In fact they are an expression of the work of God in his fullness as Father, Son and Holy Spirit. The gospel is all about our creator God's life and love incarnated in Jesus, and made available to us through the Holy Spirit.

> *There are different kinds of gifts, but the same Spirit. There are different kinds of service, but the same Lord. There are different kinds of working, but the same God works all of them in everyone.*                    (1 Corinthians 12:4–6)

Paul is saying here that through the Holy Spirit we are able to accomplish all kinds of service for our Lord Jesus, and so fulfill the will of God. This puts the gifts into their proper context. They are not given to boost our egos or even to authenticate our spiritual status. They are given to bring the kingdom of God by making his power real through us for the common good.

## Various gifts

Later in the same chapter, Paul gives a list of nine central gifts of the Holy Spirit. It is not exhaustive, but it gives us a clear idea of what the gifts are and what they are meant to do.

> *To one there is given through the Spirit the message of wisdom, to another the message of knowledge by means of the same Spirit, to another faith by the same Spirit, to another gifts of healing by that one Spirit, to another miraculous powers, to another prophecy, to another distinguishing between spirits, to another speaking in different kinds of tongues, and to still another the interpretation of tongues. All of these are the work of one and the same Spirit, and he gives them to each one, just as he determines.*                    (1 Corinthians 12:8–11)

We can describe the gifts like this:

### Message of wisdom

This gift, literally the "word of wisdom," is the very basis of our ministry to others. Without divine wisdom we find ourselves blundering into situations, making wrong judgments, taking irrelevant action and leaving a trail of misunderstanding and hurt.

God's wisdom is the ability to see things as God sees them. Through it we gain insight into the heart of a matter, so we can know what is right to do in a particular context. It may be delivered as a message to another person, but not necessarily. Words of wisdom can be received directly into our own spirit, bringing essential understanding to guide us in that moment's ministry.

## Message of knowledge

The word of knowledge also brings insight, but is more likely to be shared directly with the person concerned. By uncovering truth, it often enables much deeper areas to be touched than were previously accessible. This is Hebrews 4:12 in action:

> *For the word of God is living and active. Sharper than any double-edged sword, it penetrates even to dividing soul and spirit, joints and marrow; it judges the thoughts and attitudes of the heart.*

The gifts of wisdom and knowledge often operate together, because it takes the first to know how to handle and apply the second.

## Faith

Faith is the gift which brings assurance and confidence into our hearts. It is the power to believe in a particular situation. Through this gift we gain the certainty of what God intends to do and the expectation that this will happen.

## Gifts of healing

This word "gifts" is plural because there are many different kinds of healing for the many different illnesses and traumas which people suffer. It is not uncommon for someone to have a capacity for healing in a certain range of illness or in relation to particular emotional needs. Healing was a central part of Jesus' ministry, showing his compassion as well as his power to make us whole.

## Miraculous power

A miracle is an event which relies utterly on the supernatural intervention of God. In this category I would include the growth of missing limbs: occurrences beyond the limits of ordinary healing. The deliverances through angelic visitations that we read about in the Acts of the Apostles also count as miracles. The results they produce are signs of the extraordinary power of God.

## Prophecy

Prophetic utterance is a direct message to us, containing within it the need for a response. Agabus, for example, was a prophet in Antioch who warned the church of forthcoming famine, which historical records show occurred during the reign of Claudius in AD 49 (Acts 11:28).

Paul tells us that prophetic gifts are for the upbuilding of the whole church as well as for benefiting individuals to whom we minister:

> *Those who prophesy speak to people for their strengthening, encouragement and comfort ... those who prophesy edify the church.*                    (1 Corinthians 14:3)

## The ability to distinguish between spirits

This is the gift of discernment. John tells us in his first epistle to test the spirits and see if they are from God. By means of this gift we can distinguish between the demonic and the holy, and know what we are dealing with in any given situation.

## Different kinds of tongues

The gift of tongues – other languages, supernaturally given – is very important in equipping us for ministry. Personal exercise of this gift opens us up to the word of God, as well as to the use of other gifts. As we pray in tongues (often silently), we become more sensitive to God's will and direction in particular situations. This gift enables us to pray rightly when we would otherwise be unable to.

Paul expresses its value this way:

> *Anyone who speaks in a tongue does not speak to people but to God. Indeed, no-one understands them; they utter mysteries with their spirits* [or *by the Spirit*] ...
> *If I pray in a tongue, my spirit prays ...*
> *I thank God that I speak in tongues more than all of you.*
> (1 Corinthians 14:2, 14, 18)

### Interpretation of tongues

The gift of interpretation is needed in a corporate setting. After a message in unknown tongues is publicly given, the Spirit gives the interpretation so that everyone can understand, judge, and act on what has been said. It is not necessarily a literal translation, but more a dynamic response in English (or the language normally spoken!).

This process of hearing a word first spoken in the Spirit, and then in a known language, draws attention to the fact that God wants to speak, and heightens expectation.

## What good are the gifts?

The gifts of the Holy Spirit are of great use if handled properly. They are given to enrich our own spiritual life and release that life to others. As God brings encouragement, direction and correction among his people, the whole body of Christ can be enriched.

I find spiritual gifts essential in my own prayer life and a great help in praise and worship. Through them I can express my heart to God in a much more free and meaningful way. They stimulate my own spirit and heart.

Many people struggle with gifts such as tongues because their intellect and self-consciousness get in the way. Yet as we surrender our natural faculties to God, the new gift of praise and speech will release us from the limitations of our own thinking.

Nevertheless we are not out of control as we operate in the gifts of the Holy Spirit. The Scriptures tell us that we have a responsibility to be in control of what is happening. The Holy Spirit gives us the authority to move in the gifts while still being aware and discerning. Paul says:

> *The spirits of prophets are subject to the control of prophets. For God is not a God of disorder but of peace.*
>
> (1 Corinthians 14:32–33)

Above all, these gifts are given so that we may be a blessing to others. Notice how so many of them are used to bring God's power into the heart of other people's needs. The gifts of the Holy Spirit enable us to share the ministry of Jesus, today.

## Eagerly desire the greater gifts

It is common to begin with receiving the gift of tongues, but God desires that we go on to explore all of the gifts of the Holy Spirit. One of the signs of spiritual growth is to be continually breaking new ground in the things of God. As time passes we should enjoy a greater and greater release into the range of gifts.

Paul encourages us to *"eagerly desire spiritual gifts, especially the gift of prophecy"* (1 Corinthians 14:1). He suggests that some gifts are of more value than others, because they edify the whole body. That's why he urges the charismatic Corinthians to *"try to excel in gifts that build up the church"* (1 Corinthians 14:12).

Yet every gift of the Holy Spirit is of value and to be sought after. We can trust in God's generosity:

*If you, then, though you are evil, know how to give good gifts to your children, how much more will your Father in heaven give good gifts to those who ask him!* (Matthew 7:11)

We should be hungering after all the richness of God. Ask the Holy Spirit to equip you with his gifts!

# 6

# Now it's your turn

"Now it's your turn!"

I remember the challenge of these words vividly. They were spoken by a friend of mine, Bob Humburg, who leads a Christian center in Germany. One graduation day a new batch of students were about to leave the college and launch into a life of witness and service.

Bob reminded us simply and clearly of the fact that throughout the centuries God has had living witnesses. We know about especially noteworthy and famous Christians, but there have also been millions of unknown and unsung witnesses to the faith. "Now it's your turn," he said.

The words rang through me, bringing a new excitement about the call of God. I remembered how Mordecai spoke to Queen Esther as she hesitated to act in a national crisis. Mordecai told her that she had come to the kingdom for such an hour as this (Esther 4:14). So have we!

Before he left his disciples, Jesus foretold the Spirit's coming, and called them to be witnesses *"to the ends of the earth"* (Acts 1:8). How well these words were fulfilled in the lives of those very first believers. History confirms that these inspired men and women carried the testimony of Jesus through the then known world. It was their turn.

These words have been fulfilled to an even greater extent in succeeding generations. Despite all the failures and desertions there have been from the pure gospel, the word of Jesus has prevailed.

## Living letters

Now it's our turn! John wrote that *"in this world we are like him"* (1 John 4:17). The King James Version puts it this way: *"as he is, so are we."*

In our generation, the only living testimony that some people have is the Spirit of Jesus in our lives. Sharing him is not an option, not an optional addendum to our agenda. It is the very reason for the existence of the church.

If we reduce Jesus to a religious history lesson (knowledge without experience), he has many competitors. Yet the living power seen and felt through the lives of those who are indwelt by the Spirit of God cannot be gainsaid.

Paul used a powerful analogy to underline this when he spoke to the church at Corinth:

> *You show that you are a letter from Christ, the result of our ministry, written not with ink but with the Spirit of the living God, not on tablets of stone but on tablets of human hearts.*
>
> (2 Corinthians 3:3)

What a beautiful picture of the witness of the Spirit. He is the unmistakable inscription by which the story of Jesus is written on our lives. Because of that, the evidence of our saving God is there for all to see.

There is nothing so powerful as the testimony of a new life in Christ. For many who never enter a church or read the Bible, our lives will be the most immediate witness to the power of God they may come in contact with. We may be the first "Bibles" that many people ever read.

## The Spirit helps us

Many people freeze up at the thought of being called to share their experience of God. Perhaps this has to do with our preconceptions of "witnessing." Yet personal witness does not depend on expertise but on our daily openness to God. It is not preaching or even giving a public testimony, but a matter of letting our whole lives be the arena in which we allow God to work.

Through this we allow the Holy Spirit to flow like living water from deep within us, just as Jesus said (John 7:38–39). In this way the reality and love of God will touch the lives of people with whom we are in contact.

## Experience

Our testimony grows out of our experience of Christ. There is no real, vital truth apart from *experienced* truth. This does not mean, however, that experience is the arbiter of truth! Some things remain true whether or not we experience them. For example, it remains true that Christ died for my sin whether or not I personally experience it. But it is not effective in me unless I do experience it.

It is our experience of the truth that makes it real and powerful in our lives. That is what Jesus meant when he said that we would know the truth, and the truth would set us free (John 8:32).

This is at the very heart of discipleship. A disciple follows the truth not as a mere philosophy or ideology, but as a life-changing reality. This can only happen through a personal relationship of faith and commitment with the one who described himself as the way, the truth and the life.

There is a big difference between a person who can repeat facts about Jesus, and one who can say with conviction, "I know." Paul spoke in such a way when he wrote to Timothy:

> *I am not ashamed, because I know whom I have believed, and am convinced that he is able to guard what I have entrusted to him for that day.* (2 Timothy 1:12)

The Holy Spirit makes this experience of God possible for us. He makes the forgiveness and freedom of Christ real within our lives, and releases God's power to enable us to live in the kingdom of God. This is why the process of conversion and commitment is so important. Through it we consciously turn away from an old way of life and enter into a new life in Christ.

Ask yourself what you know of God. Examine your spiritual experience. How have you known the help of the Holy Spirit in the circumstances of your life? What have you witnessed of the saving power of God? The material for our personal testimonies is built into the very fiber of our own experience of life with Christ.

## Assurance

The Holy Spirit is a witness, first and foremost. He witnesses to Jesus, revealing the meaning of his life, death and resurrection. Jesus spoke of this as the great work of the Holy Spirit:

> *But when he, the Spirit of truth, comes, he will guide you into all truth. He will not speak on his own; he will speak only what he hears ... He will bring glory to me by taking what is mine and making it known to you.*                    (John 16:13–14)

The Holy Spirit is also a witness within us of our own status in Christ. This is the ground of our assurance as believers. Paul underlines this truth when he says:

> *The Spirit himself testifies with our spirit that we are God's children.*                                        (Romans 8:16)

In his letter to the Ephesians, Paul makes a similar point, speaking of the Spirit as a deposit which is the guarantee of even greater things to come. The original Greek word for *deposit* also means "engagement ring." So Paul is using the metaphor of a ring given between two lovers to symbolize the certainty of God's commitment to us.

*Having believed, you were marked in him with a seal, the promised Holy Spirit, who is a deposit guaranteeing our inheritance until the redemption of those who are God's possession.*

(Ephesians 1:13–14)

Effective personal witness should not be filled with tension and anxiety. Instead, it should bear witness to the relationship of confidence and trust that exists between Christ and his bride.

## Boldness

One of the outstanding features of the book of Acts is the freedom with which the early Christians testified to Christ. One word, *boldness*, crops up time and time again in verses such as this:

*Now, Lord, consider their threats and enable your servants to speak your word with great boldness.* (Acts 4:29)

The disciples spoke and acted with a boldness that did not come from themselves, but was the result of the work of the Holy Spirit within their hearts. This boldness did not grow out of arrogance or aggression. The true meaning of the original Greek word has nothing to do with such attitudes. This is highlighted later by Paul:

*Pray also for me, that whenever I open my mouth, words may be given me so that I will fearlessly make known the mystery of the gospel.* (Ephesians 6:19)

Jesus had promised his disciples that they need not have any fear when they were called to give an account of themselves on his behalf. The words they were to speak would be given to them in the very moment they needed them. And the book of Acts bears eloquent witness to the fact that the Holy Spirit gives both words and power to those who would stand for Jesus.

Sometimes evangelism is considered a matter of personality types, as though only the extroverted are called to it. It is true, of course, that God uses our diverse personalities in diverse ways. There are people whom you will reach at a personal level whom I could never touch, and vice versa. However, spiritual boldness is not to do with natural extraversion, but to openness to God in every situation.

## Understanding

Some people are afraid to share their faith in God with others because they lack confidence in their own understanding of the gospel. They feel they don't know enough to be able to handle questions or difficulties that may arise.

I remember suffering from the same syndrome when I was in business. One part of my job was to give presentations to medical teams on the latest drugs my firm had produced. It was fine when I was well acquainted with every aspect of the product, but if something had prevented me from being fully prepared, I lost my confidence. I would feel anxious in case the conversation should lead me into areas where my ignorance would become apparent.

There are two simple steps that you can take to deal with this fear. First, start where you are. A testimony is simply to do with what you have witnessed about God within your own life. Satan will try to paralyze us with fear about questions that people may well not be interested in anyway. Most people don't want a theological treatise!

There is a story in the gospels of a man who was healed of blindness. The enemies of Jesus interrogated him, trying to trap him with arguments that went far beyond his experience. In the end, the man exclaimed what he knew for certain:

> *One thing I do know. I was blind but now I see!* (John 9:25)

You know something that no one else knows: what God has done for you in Christ and through the power of the Holy Spirit.

The second thing is to determine to move on from where you are. You will be amazed at how much you can grow in your understanding if you spend time with the Scriptures. The Holy Spirit himself is your teacher. Paul reminds us of the help that is offered to us:

> *We have not received the spirit of the world but the Spirit who is from God, that we may understand what God has freely given us. This is what we speak, not in words taught us by human wisdom but in words taught by the Spirit, expressing spiritual truths in spiritual words.* (1 Corinthians 2:12–13)

Today there are a multitude of helps available to increase our knowledge. Seminars, books, tapes, videos and computer resources can support us in moving forward in the things of God. For most of us it is a matter of will, not intellectual or spiritual capacity. We need to be willing to give our time and minds to the Lord, leaving aside some of the trivia that would otherwise fill our lives.

## Capability

There is nowhere that the gifts of the Holy Spirit are more relevant than in the area of witness. The Holy Spirit not only gives us the power to speak, but through his gifts of wisdom and discernment shows us when and how to speak into any particular situation.

We have a great commission to go and make disciples of all nations, but we are not left to ourselves in the task. Jesus promised his first disciples that he would always be with them. Through the enabling power of the Spirit, he is always with us, giving us power and guidance in our witness to him.

## Opportunity

One thing that we see in the book of Acts is the way that the Holy Spirit leads believers into areas of effective witness. He takes the initiative, opening the right doors to where he has prepared the ground for the reception of the gospel.

One of the clearest examples of this is the experience of Philip, who is told by the angel of the Lord to take the road south to the desert. On the way he meets the Ethiopian official who is primed to listen to the testimony that Philip has for him (see Acts 8).

Another case is when Peter is led by a powerful dream to share the message of Christ with the gentile Cornelius. This event had a major effect on the spread of the gospel throughout the world (see Acts 10).

Paul's whole ministry was directed this way and he became very open to the Spirit's leading in every circumstance. Even when he was thrown into jail at Philippi, he was ready to recognize the hand of God, and ended up leading his jailer to faith in Christ. Later, writing from house arrest in Rome to the same Philippians, he reminded them that the things that had happened to him had served to advance the cause of the gospel (Philippians 1:12).

It will be like this for us if we open ourselves to the possibilities in each situation. Life takes on a new dimension altogether when we follow the leading of the Spirit each day. We will be surprised at how many opportunities we are given to share our faith in Jesus.

This does not mean that we need to be always straining for a conversational opening, or barging into people's lives. We follow the Lord as he gives opportunities. Sometimes witness means making a clear statement about what we believe and why. Often it means demonstrating God's love through our attitudes and concern for other people. We follow God's leading because it is all about honoring him:

> *For we do not preach ourselves, but Jesus Christ as Lord, and ourselves as your servants for Jesus' sake.*  (2 Corinthians 4:5)

## Love

It is the love of God that compels us to be his witnesses. We are not driven by fear, guilt, competition or condemnation. All these have been removed through the forgiving power of his love. Because we have come to know the reality of God's love in our own hearts and lives, we want as many others as possible to share the same gift:

> *For Christ's love compels us, because we are convinced that one died for all.* (2 Corinthians 5:14)

People feel the authenticity of love like this. It is more than the love that rises from our own human nature; it is a result of God's work in our hearts. Paul reminded the early church that this love is poured out into our hearts by the Holy Spirit (Romans 5:5). The power of this love transforms our testimony into something more than words:

> *This is how we know what love is: Jesus Christ laid down his life for us. And we ought to lay down our lives for one another. ... Dear children, let us not love with words or tongue but with actions and in truth.* (1 John 3:16, 18)

## The healing of the nations

Ezekiel ended his great prophecy with a tremendous vision of the renewing power of God. He pictured it as water flowing out from the temple. The further this water flows, the deeper it becomes, making the sea water fresh and bringing life to all creatures. It is a great river of life flowing out of the heart of God:

> *Fruit trees of all kinds will grow on both banks of the river. Their leaves will not wither, nor will their fruit fail. Every month they will bear, because the water from the sanctuary flows to them. Their fruit will serve for food and their leaves for healing.* (Ezekiel 47:12)

This is an image of what our lives should be. Fed by the flowing water of the Holy Spirit of God, they will produce his fruit so that we become a source of life and healing for those we encounter day by day.

# 7

# Meeting God at the dead end

The secret of being filled with the power of the Holy Spirit is to know our poverty without it. We need to know that we need it!

For two years or so before I was baptized in the Spirit, I went through a time of deep heart searching. The confusion of my mind and spirit led almost to a sense of desperation. When I met people who were evidently living in a reality of God that I lacked, there was a great longing in me to have what they had.

## Four steps

There are four simple fundamentals that will help us to receive.

### Thirst

God deals with thirsty people. He will bless those whose hearts are really after him and who unreservedly allow him to work in their lives.

Time and again the Scriptures invite those who are thirsty to come and drink of the water of life (Isaiah 55:1; Psalm 107:35–36). Jesus himself said that whoever was thirsty should come to him and drink (John 4:10–14). His word in the Revelation to John was,

> *Let those who are thirsty come; and let all who wish take the free gift of the water of life.* (Revelation 22:17)

Let God work within you, to stir up a thirst and desire for something more. Seek him with all your heart and you will surely find the Holy Spirit releasing the living water of God's life and power in your inner being.

## Openness

Be willing and open for God to do in you whatever he desires to do. This is the greatest struggle for many people. We are instinctively resistant to change! Circumstances, habits, tradition, prejudices as well as pure laziness condition us against being open to a new move from God.

All of us have factors within our lifestyles and personalities which militate against our giving ourselves away to God. He challenges this, and sometimes there will be a battle in the area of our will as God seeks to open us to the possibility of change.

## Receptivity

Jesus himself invites us first to ask and then to receive. Throughout the Scriptures we are encouraged to actively reach out and accept from God the good things he has for every one of us in Jesus. This may involve a readiness to step out in faith, even when we are unsure.

God can be trusted! James says:

> *Every good and perfect gift is from above, coming down from the Father of the heavenly lights, who does not change like shifting shadows.* (James 1:17)

## Obedience

Knowing the touch of God on your life is only the first step. The harder thing is following it through in the days and years that follow. But the Holy Spirit who initially fills us with the power of God continues to work in our lives.

We have the responsibility of following and fulfilling God's call for us, but the power and strength to do it comes from the Holy Spirit. Paul encouraged the church in the same way:

> *Continue to work out your salvation with fear and trembling, for it is God who works in you to will and to act according to his good purpose.* (Philippians 2:12–13)

## Return empty

Two outstanding incidents always come to mind when I speak to people about being filled with the Holy Spirit.

The first is the testimony of a man that I met shortly before I was baptized in the Spirit. He was a theological teacher in a university, as well as a monk who had committed himself to a life of simplicity.

I was a university chaplain at the time, and hundreds of students were finding the power of God in a new way. It has to be honestly stated that none of it had much to do with us chaplains! To understand this phenomenon, we invited this man to come and speak to us about the book of Acts.

When this theological monk arrived, he didn't so much give the lecture as to *be* the lecture! It was quite evident that he knew something firsthand. His testimony astounded us and challenged me deeply.

The man told us that he had been an ordained priest for many years and had taught in one of the most prestigious theological faculties in Scotland. But over some time he had become progressively disturbed by an awareness of a great spiritual lack in his own life. In the end, his desperation of spirit drove him to contact a lifelong friend of his, who at that time happened to be the Archbishop of Canterbury.

The Archbishop invited his friend to go down to Canterbury and meet with him. But he never got quite as far as that.

The man took a seat on the night train out of Edinburgh, and as he traveled on his way, he became darker and darker in his spirit. The train was just approaching the station at York when he cried out for God to speak to him. He felt totally empty and bereft of joy.

At that moment a goods train made up of box wagons came in the opposite direction. As he stared out of the window at the other train slowly pulling past, the last wagon suddenly came into view. There in large chalk letters was the word of God to his spirit on the side of the box van. It was the instruction to the shunt yard but it came to him as the pure divine word. It said, "Return empty to Scotland."

That's how he felt, and that's what he did. He got off the train, went back up north and there he met God in a completely new way through the baptism of the Holy Spirit. It revolutionized his life, and the effects of it made a great impact on the rest of us that day.

## The dead end

The second incident is very different but carries the same message.

My wife and I once took a brief holiday on a narrow-boat along one of the English canals. It was October, a quiet time of the year, and the fun of negotiating the canal locks was a new experience for me.

As we entered one of the deepest locks in the canal system, it suddenly struck me that we were seeing a living parable of the ways of God with us.

To make progress through a lock, a series of steps is necessary. You cannot go forward until you go into an "empty" lock and close the gates behind you. Then the sluice gates need to be wound open so that water from above can enter into the lock and raise the boat to a new level. Finally the gates in front need to be opened so that the vessel can proceed on the next stage of the journey.

Now, what was described as an "empty" lock clearly had enough water to float the boat. There just wasn't enough to take it further up the system. Isn't that just like our lives? Often we know something of God and his power. It has blessed us up until the present, and yet it seems it's not enough to get us any further. We have to go in and shut the door on all that is past before we can experience that tremendous new infill of the Holy Spirit.

Notice that so often God brings us to emptiness and a seeming dead end before he is able to fill us with the living water of the Spirit. This may sound simplistic, but it rings true for many people.

Don't be afraid of what God may do. Love, not fear, is the key to the work of the Holy Spirit. The New King James Version puts it this way:

> *For God has not given us a spirit of fear, but a spirit of power and of love and of a sound mind.*     (2 Timothy 1:7)

Open yourself to God. Let the wind of the Holy Spirit blow through you. Be open to receive all he gives you.

Let him sanctify you through and through – spirit, soul and body. Receive from him the gifts he brings, and learn how to praise, worship and witness in the power of God.

It may help you to ask someone who knows what it means to be filled with the Holy Spirit to pray with you. But you can ask for yourself, right now. Use a simple prayer like the one on the next page, and pray with faith. The Father will hear you and answer you in the power of his Spirit.

*Dear Father,*
*Thank you for the promise that whoever asks will receive*
   *and whoever seeks will find.*
*I know that I need your power in my life.*
*I know that I need more of the fruit of the Holy Spirit, too.*
*Lord, I confess my sin and ask you to cleanse me through*
   *the blood of Jesus.*
*Please fill me to overflowing with your Holy Spirit.*
*I open myself now, and reach out to receive all that*
   *you have to give me.*
*I thank you, praise and worship you for your love and*
   *goodness.*
*Hallelujah!*
*Amen.*